SERENITY SPACE
Adult Coloring Book

Mandala Coloring Book for Anxiety, Mindfulness, Creativity, and
Stress Relief

Markyia Nichols, MD aka DrKyia

This Book Belongs To:

_____

Guidelines for Using This Book

- Please be sure to use soft colored pencils to get the best results

- If you are using gel pens or markers, we recommend putting a piece of card stock behind the image you are working on in order to prevent bleed-through

- This mandala book is designed to get you into the relaxing alpha and theta brainwaves. Therefore, repeating swirls and patterns in a particular image are common, although each design is unique in itself

- Be sure to color the ones you resonate with in the moment. Choose the image that "draws" you to it.

- Relax...and enjoy!!

**Did you enjoy these mandalas? Ready for more?

I would love to gift you more coloring pages, for FREE. Just
drop me a line and tell me how you liked the coloring book.

Please send your thoughts to support@drkyia.com and I will
send you even more relaxing images to color.

A SPECIAL THANK YOU TO MY READERS...

Want even more? I always have special content and bonuses exclusively for those on my mailing list.

If you are already on my mailing list, you don't need to do anything extra. Please drop me a line at support@drkyia.com to let me know how you liked Serenity Space

Not yet a member? What are you waiting for then?! In addition to all the juicy bonuses I give out, you will be the first to know about FREE giveaways, uplifting content, and anything NEW the second it hits!

Go to www.drkyia.com to sign up right away and receive a bonus recipe that will have your entire family salivating!!

ABOUT DRKYIA

Markyia Nichols, MD aka DrKyia is a Johns Hopkins trained, board certified ob/gyn, author and functional medicine expert who is committed to integrating the physical, mental, emotional, and spiritual components of health.

After complete burnout following her training, and almost retiring from medicine because she was tired of treating "symptoms" and never getting true healing for her patients, she started exploring other healing methods. She was determined to find tools for herself and her patients that would heal disease rather than putting a band-aid over it. She clearly recognized the gaps within the traditional medicine modality and began exploring ways to treat the entire person, taking into consideration the emotional and spiritual aspects of health.

She came to realize that the missing piece of the puzzle involved identifying the root cause of disease, not just on a physical level, but also on the emotional and spiritual level. Unless this is holistically addressed, issues simply re-manifest, never resolve or get worse.
Her mission is to assist people to "remember" who they really are, which is much more than our physical bodies. As we heal all aspects of ourselves, our bodies and lives come into balance and flow more harmoniously.

When DrKyia isn't assisting clients to heal from the inside out and feel their best, she can be found coloring, spending time in nature, cooking yummy healthy desserts (she's got a sweet tooth), or playing with her honey and fur baby. You can find her at www.drkyia.com or hanging out on instagram @drkyia

Made in the USA
Middletown, DE
18 October 2022

13002890R00066